my pet *remembrance* journal

by Enid Traisman M.S.W.

A **DoveLewis Emergency Animal Hospital** Publication

Sponsored by **Dignified Pet Services**

Photographers: Alicia Dickerson of Four-Legged Photo
Michael Jones Photography Studio

Project Manager: Tiffini Mueller
Creative Director: Michelle Leal
Design & Illustration by Lisa Adza

PHOTO BY ALICIA DICKERSON, FOUR-LEGGED PHOTO

Dignified Pet Services Founders and Owners
Michael Remsing (right), Randy Tjaden (left) and Avani

"For Those Who Deal With Our Friends the Animals

We Ask a Heart of Compassion, Gentle Hands and Kindly Words"

ALBERT SCHWEITZER

A Dignified Story

We all know that Oregonians love their pets—in fact, in Oregon, pets are family too!

That's why people who lose their pet companions deserve the same compassion, respect and tender care as those who lose a human companion. This is the simple, but solid foundation that Dignified Pet Services was founded on and thrives on today. The founders of Dignified Pet Services, Michael Remsing and Randy Tjaden, understand this philosophy because of a lifetime dedication to helping those who lose a human companion or other family member. As Funeral Directors, funeral home owners and pet lovers, Michael and Randy could see the tremendous needs of those losing pet companions and more importantly, they were in a unique position to address those needs through their vast background in funeral service. Dignified Pet Services is a full service funeral home and cremation center specifically dedicated to caring for pets and the people who love them so dearly.

The DoveLewis Partnership

Soon after opening the doors of Dignified Pet Services in 2000, a partnership between DoveLewis & Dignified Pet Services emerged. The relationship was a natural one based on the common philosophies of DoveLewis and Dignified Pet Services. DoveLewis was founded on the belief that pet companions and their families deserve human quality emergency care and Dignified Pet Services was founded on the belief that pet companions and their families deserve human quality aftercare, so the relationship between the two was cemented.

Today, Dignified Pet Services is the primary supporter of the DoveLewis Pet Loss Support Program. This relationship benefits all those who experience the loss of a pet companion—the Pet Loss Support Program and Enid Traisman, the program founder and director, are here to provide support and understanding while Dignified Pet Services is here to provide compassionate care and dignified service.

I must admit, I was quite honored when I was asked to write the Foreword for the new release of Enid's Pet Remembrance Journal.

When we opened Dignified Pet Services back in October of 2000, I reached out to every pet lover that I knew and asked for guidance. A friend gave me Enid Traisman's phone number and told me about the DoveLewis Pet Loss Support Program that Enid had founded in 1986 and continues to direct.

I called Enid and could tell from the moment we first spoke that there would be a special bond between us. Enid invited me to attend her Pet Loss Support group and I was amazed by the number of people attending as well as the unique way in which each person was dealing with their grief. While attending my first meeting I was privileged to receive my own copy of Enid's Pet Remembrance Journal; I found her Journal to be a wonderful resource.

While attending the Pet Loss Support Group over the months ahead, I was able to see first-hand how people have grown and have worked their way through the grief process. What I saw was a true testament of how fortunate we are in the Portland/Metropolitan area to have a resource like Enid and The Pet Loss Support Program.

I am an avid supporter of the DoveLewis Pet Loss Support Program. I have seen hundreds of people over the last 10 years, benefit immensely from their time with Enid and the Pet Loss Support Group. I'm not sure where these folks would have turned for help if not for Enid and her devotion and dedication to people who have experienced the loss of a dearly loved pet companion.

Michael Remsing

CO-OWNER & FOUNDER,
DIGNIFIED PET SERVICES

Shakespeare, in his play Much Ado About Nothing, points out that "Any person can manage grief, but he who has it." None of us know what the "right" way to grieve is, yet we all engage in this process when a significant attachment is disrupted by loss. Enid Traisman, MSW, has added a new tool that can be used to get through the bereavement, mourning, and grief following the loss of a pet. That pets are significant in many of our lives is non-refutable. They offer us protection, companionship, humor, and unconditional love. The loss of a pet is experienced by many in ways analogous to the loss of a human significant other and in many cases, to an even greater level.

My Pet Remembrance Journal is a sensitive, thorough, effective adjunct in assisting those going through pet loss related grief. The book reminds us what normal grief is about and how not to be ashamed of those feelings. It provides opportunities for nostalgic memories that we know are so important in the mastering of grief. The book provides an opportunity to memorialize, remember, and to move on when ready. This book is mandatory for those going through this extremely difficult time in their lives. Children, adolescents, and adults of all ages will benefit from Ms. Traisman's insight into pet loss.

Herbert Nieburg, Ph.D.

AUTHOR OF *PET LOSS: A THOUGHTFUL GUIDE FOR ADULTS AND CHILDREN*

FOUR WINDS HOSPITAL • KATONAH, N.Y. • HARPER COLLINS

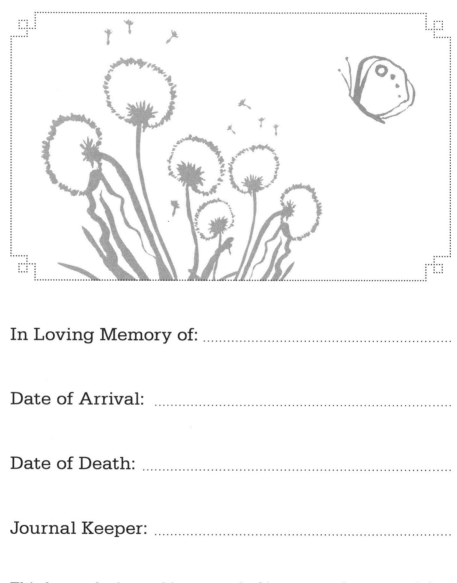

In Loving Memory of: ....

Date of Arrival: ....

Date of Death: ....

Journal Keeper: ....

This keepsake journal is a record of important facts, special thoughts and warmest memories. The purpose of this book is to enhance your healing process and honor your relationship with your pet.

Contents

This Remembrance Journal is expressly for you. It is a special place for you to share the feelings that have arisen since the death of your beloved pet. Here you can write down your thoughts and feelings that are ever-present and ever-changing. In your journal you can privately go over the details of your loss and its effect on you.

Your reaction to the death of your pet is as unique and individual as was your relationship. Your personal grief reaction is affected by your experience with previous losses, how closely bonded you were to your pet, cause of death, support system and your personal nature. My hope is that this guided journal will help you with the challenging journey ahead of you.

There are no shortcuts or specific steps to follow to make grieving quicker or less painful. The strength of the bond you had with your pet often serves as a barometer for the intensity of the grief you feel. Experiencing the pain of your loss is an essential part of working through and integrating your grief.

You never forget. You received a lot from your pet and will always have in your heart the love he or she gave to you. Know that there is no perfect way to grieve. There is no wrong way to use your journal. It is here for you to express your thoughts and feelings. You can use it to help you experience, explore and understand the emotional roller coaster you are on. You do not have to complete every sentence or fill every space. Use only those that feel right for you. Sometimes you will have a lot to write, other times you may just want to read and think. Write in any area that touches your heart at the moment, even if it is in the middle or end of the journal. There are extra pages at the end of each chapter for keepsakes. Be creative, use colored pens, pencils, and markers, glue in pictures and meaningful clippings. Personalize your journal so that it intimately reflects you and your pet and all that you have shared together.

Enid Traisman

NORMAL GRIEF RESPONSE AFTER THE DEATH OF YOUR PET

What you might feel after the death

- Shock/numbness
- Denial
- Anger/guilt
- Regret
- Relief
- Depression

Reasons why it may hurt so much when a pet dies

- Your pet is a source of unconditional love and appreciation
- A pet becomes part of who your are; an alter-ego, child and/or companion
- Many times, places, feelings, thoughts and events are associated with your pet
- Your pet did things just for you and you did things just for your pet
- Each of you gave the other a great deal of emotional support
- Losing your pet is like losing part of yourself

Possible Physical Responses

- Crying
- Dry mouth, difficulty in swallowing
- No appetite or over–eating
- Sleep disturbances
- Aching heart, chest pains and/or an empty hollow feeling
- Lack of energy and motivation
- Unable to concentrate, forgetfulness
- Sensitivity to loud noises

Possible Emotional Responses

- Everything reminds your of your pet, you may experience seeing or hearing your pet
- Feeling distanced from others, as if no one understands or cares
- Questioning the meaning of life and mortality, reevaluating your priorities in life
- Worrying about others you love dying
- Afraid to love again, fear of the pain of loss

SOFTENING THE PAIN

- Talking, talking, talking… To family, friends, coworkers, a support group and/or counselor
- Writing about your pet and about your feelings in a journal
- Creating a funeral/memorial service, sharing memories, and sharing your pain
- Be extra kind to yourself: get a massage, a bubble bath, exercise, visit with friends
- Set up a memorial in your pet's honor
- Create a ritual and repeat it every year

THE LABOR OF MOURNING

It is called the labor of mourning because it is exhausting and difficult work to grieve over the loss of a loved one. The "work" is actually feeling the pain that you experience whenever you think of or are reminded of your pet who is no longer with you. Healthy grieving is going through the pain. It is a typical response to try avoiding the pain. In the long run, that may make things worse. The pain of the loss will soften in time if you acknowledge it. Yes, pain hurts and it is uncomfortable, but it's not bad; it is a testimony of the love and joy you shared with your pet.

Our animals shepherd us through certain eras of our lives.

When we are ready to turn the corner and make it on our own...

They let us go.

SUPPORT GROUP WISDOM

The story of how, when and where we met each other:

The Date: ....

The City and State: ....

Describe the circumstances, your feelings, reactions, intuitions, and first impressions.

....

....

....

....

....

....

....

....

....

....

....

....

....

....

....

....

What I know about your personal history:

What breed(s) were your parents? Were you planned? How many were in your litter?

Did you come from a breeder, shelter, pet shop or other? ....

....

....

....

....

....

....

....

....

....

....

....

....

....

....

....

....

What you looked like, felt like, smelled like when I was first able to be with you:

....

....

....

....

....

....

....

....

....

....

Your unique and notable personality traits: ....

....

....

....

....

....

....

We Named You ....

How long did it take to come up with your name? Other ideas we had? Why this is

the name we chose and how it fit your looks and/or personality. ....

....

....

....

....

....

....

....

....

Nicknames and Endearments: ....

....

....

....

....

....

....

....

Chapter 2 YOUR PERSONAL SPACE & BELONGINGS

Color of your collar, tags and leash: ....

....

....

....

....

What your ID tag said: ....

....

....

....

....

Favorite appropriate toys: ....

....

....

....

....

Favorite inappropriate toys: ....

....

....

....

....

Favorite treats: ....

....

....

....

....

Where you slept / where you were supposed to sleep: ....

....

....

....

....

....

....

Any unusual or specific preferences: ....

....

....

....

....

....

Chapter 3 LOOKING BACK AT THE EARLY YEARS

Funny, cute and memorable stories and pictures: ....

....

....

....

....

....

....

....

....

....

....

....

....

....

....

....

....

....

....

....

....

What your typical day was like: ....

....

....

....

....

....

....

....

....

....

....

....

....

....

....

....

....

....

....

....

....

The greeting you gave me when I would return home: ....

....

....

....

....

....

....

....

....

....

....

What we enjoyed doing together most: ....

....

....

....

....

....

....

Chapter 4 AS OUR LIVES & ROUTINES EVOLVED

Places we loved to walk: ....

....

....

....

....

....

....

....

....

People and animals we loved visiting with: ....

....

....

....

....

....

....

....

....

....

....

Comments people would make about you: ....

....

....

....

....

....

....

....

....

How you let me know what you wanted: ....

....

....

....

....

....

....

....

....

Chapter 4 AS OUR LIVES & ROUTINES EVOLVED

Favorite games we played: ....

....

....

....

....

....

....

....

....

....

....

....

....

....

....

....

....

....

....

....

....

Tricks I taught you, and tricks you taught me: ....

Chapter 4 AS OUR LIVES & ROUTINES EVOLVED

Things that you did not like at all: ....

....

....

....

....

....

....

....

....

....

....

....

Mischievous things you did and why: ....

....

....

....

....

....

....

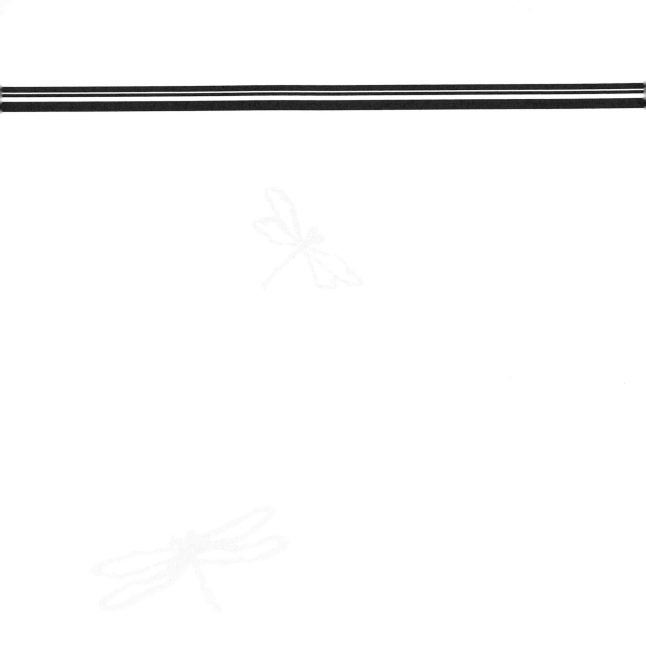

Vacations we took together and how we got there: ....

....

....

....

....

....

....

....

....

....

....

....

....

Who took care of you when I went away and could not bring you along: ....

....

....

....

....

How we celebrated holidays: ....

....

....

....

....

....

....

....

....

....

....

....

....

....

....

....

....

....

....

All that we've shared
is woven in my heart.

Each thread is a memory
From which I will never part.

Include details about our emotional, physical, intuitive, psychic, therapeutic connection.

Chapter 6 OUR SPECIAL BOND

In so many ways we met each other's needs: ....

....

....

....

....

....

....

....

....

....

....

....

....

....

....

....

....

....

....

You were by my side during these major life events that were joyful and/or painful:

....

....

....

....

....

....

....

....

Special things that I did for you: ....

....

....

....

....

....

....

....

Mementos

What you thought of your Veterinarian, examination and shots: ....

....

....

....

....

....

....

....

....

What I thought of your Veterinarian: ....

....

....

....

....

....

....

....

....

....

....

Document important medical information here: ....

....

....

....

....

....

....

....

....

....

....

....

....

....

....

....

....

....

Mementos

Here is a description of the last weeks and days of your life as I now recall them:

....
....
....
....
....
....
....
....
....
....
....
....
....
....
....
....
....
....
....
....

Special "last time" events that we shared: ....

....

....

....

....

....

....

....

....

....

....

....

....

....

....

....

....

....

....

....

Difficult decisions I made and why: ....

....

....

....

....

....

....

....

....

....

....

....

....

....

....

....

....

....

....

Why I was or was not with you when you died, and what it was like: ....

....

....

....

....

....

....

....

....

....

Why I chose to see you/be with your body after your death,

or why I chose not to, and how I feel about it: ....

....

....

....

....

....

....

....

....

Chapter 8 THE END OF YOUR LIFE

If I could rewrite the last days of your life, this is how it would be: ....

....

....

....

....

....

....

....

....

....

....

....

....

....

....

....

....

....

....

....

....

....

Mementos

43

Chapter 9 DISPOSITION OF YOUR REMAINS

I choose between burial or cremation. This is what I chose and why:.................................

....

....

....

....

....

....

....

....

....

....

If I placed special items with your body, they were significant and symbolic because:

....

....

....

....

....

....

....

....

Your final resting place is: ....

....

....

....

This place was chosen because: ....

....

....

....

....

....

....

....

Others who were with me, or why I chose to be alone for our final farewell: ....

....

....

....

....

....

....

Special things I said or did, or wish I had: ....

....

....

....

....

....

....

....

....

Choices I've made regarding your personal belongings: ....

....

....

....

....

....

....

....

....

....

These items I will keep and cherish forever:

Mementos

My pain over the loss of you is sometimes physical. This it how it feels: ....

....

....

....

....

....

....

....

....

....

These are the painful emotions that drain me: ....

....

....

....

....

....

....

....

....

The times of day that are hardest for me are: ....

....

....

....

....

....

....

....

....

....

These things I cannot bear to do yet: ....

....

....

....

....

....

....

....

Chapter 10 THE LABOR OF MOURNING

Late at night, when the world is fast asleep, I'm awake thinking about: ....

....

....

....

....

....

....

....

This is what is most difficult about coming home: ....

....

....

....

....

....

....

....

....

....

....

This is what is comforting about being home:

....

....

....

....

....

....

....

....

....

There have been jolting reminders of your death:

....

....

....

....

....

....

....

....

There are times when I have an unexpected stab of pain: ....

....

....

....

....

....

....

There are times when I feel unexpected happiness: ....

....

....

....

....

There are times I think I hear you, see you, or feel your presence. This is how I

interpret and feel about this phenomenon: ....

....

....

....

....

....

What I miss most about you right now: ....

....

....

....

....

....

....

....

....

....

....

....

....

....

....

....

....

....

....

"*I* CAN'T HELP THINKING, 'IF ONLY' AND 'WHY DID I?' OR 'WHY DIDN'T I?'."

Things I regret and feel guilty about: ....

....

....

....

....

....

....

....

....

....

....

....

....

....

....

....

....

....

....

What I am sorry for: ....

....

....

....

....

....

....

....

In my heart I know that I would never intentionally have harmed you. I know I must

forgive myself as you would forgive me. This is what I am doing to work toward

forgiving myself so that I can lessen my grief and continue to heal: ....

....

....

....

....

....

....

....

....

Chapter 10 THE LABOR OF MOURNING

"NEW GRIEF AWAKENS THE OLD." —THOMAS FULLER

Other losses I have experienced and when those losses occurred: ....

....

....

....

....

....

....

....

My feelings at the time and how I coped: ....

....

....

....

....

....

....

....

....

How my feelings are different and similar over the loss of you: ....

....

....

....

....

....

....

....

....

....

....

....

....

....

....

....

....

....

....

....

Mementos

You don't heal from a loss
because time passes,

You heal because of what you
do with the time

People I can talk to: ....

....

....

....

....

Places I feel comfortable crying: ....

....

....

....

....

Ways of pampering myself: ....

....

....

....

....

....

Creative expressions of my love and loss: ....

....

....

....

....

Chapter 11 GRIEVING IN A HEALTHY WAY

"*I* AM LEARNING TO ACCEPT THAT GRIEF AFFECTS ALL AREAS OF MY LIFE.
I CAN'T DO EVERYTHING AS WELL AS I DID BEFORE."

Inability to concentrate: ....

....

....

....

Lack of motivation: ....

....

....

....

Low energy level: ....

....

....

....

Lack of focus: ....

....

....

....

Sleep patterns are disturbed. This is what I am doing to ensure I get enough sleep:

....

....

....

Eating patterns are different. This is what I am doing to keep my diet healthy:

....

....

....

Physical activity releases endorphins, which are healing agents. This is the exercise

routine I am trying to do to keep my body healthy during this stressful, painful time:

....

....

....

I am learning to recognize when I am avoiding facing my pain.

These are the signals I get: ....

....

....

....

....

....

If someone listens,
or stretches out a hand,

or whispers a kind word
of encouragement,

or attempts to understand
a lonely person,

extraordinary things
begin to happen.

SHARED AT A SUPPORT GROUP

"GRIEF SHARED IS GRIEF DIMINISHED."

Talking to family: ....

....

....

....

....

Talking to friends: ....

....

....

....

....

Journaling: ....

....

....

....

....

Attending a Pet Loss Support Group:...

....

....

....

....

"LIFE IS FAITH, WHETHER WE RECOGNIZE IT OR NOT."

My beliefs about being reunited are: ....

....

....

....

....

....

....

....

....

....

....

....

....

....

....

....

....

....

My dreams about you: ....

....

....

....

....

....

....

....

....

....

....

....

....

....

....

....

....

....

"*M*EMORIALIZING IS THE ART OF CREATING SPECIAL WAYS OF REMEMBERING YOUR PET."

This is what is inscribed in my heart and on your final resting place: ....

....

....

....

In your memory, donations have been and will be made to: ....

....

....

....

....

In your memory, I have developed the following rituals which help me feel close to you:

....

....

....

To recognize your absence and keep your memory alive during special holidays

and anniversaries, I will:..

....

....

....

....

I first thought of you with happiness and not pain when: ....

....

....

....

....

....

I first laughed and felt good when: ....

....

....

....

....

I made a conscious decision to triumph over my grief when: ....

....

....

....

I can look at your picture, have a memory and visit a special place sometimes

without crying: ....

....

....

....

....

"Although death is an ending, it is also a beginning. Death has much to teach us about living."

What I have learned about myself since your death: ....

....

....

....

....

....

....

....

How my priorities in life have changed: ....

....

....

....

....

....

....

....

....

....

Things I was never aware of before but am aware of now: ....

....

....

....

....

....

I now recognize these strengths in myself that I didn't before: ....

....

....

....

....

....

Changes I am making in my life as a result of loving you and grieving over your death:

....

....

....

....

....

Chapter 11 GRIEVING IN A HEALTHY WAY

What did your pet find most lovable about you? ....

....

....

....

Describe these lasting gifts you received as a result

of having such a special relationship with your pet:

To love unconditionally: ....

....

....

To be more accepting of yourself: ....

....

....

To be true to yourself in times of crisis and doubt: ....

....

....

Wisdom: ....

....

....

Courage: ....

....

....

Forgiveness: ....
....
....

Spontaneity: ....
....
....

To give yourself over to love: ....
....
....

To be open to joy: ....
....
....

To communicate love: ....
....
....

To grow in humility: ....
....
....

This is how i acknowledge these lasting gifts you left with me: ....
....
....

Mementos

Chapter 12 MY GOODBYE LETTER

There is a bridge connecting Heaven and Earth. It is called The Rainbow Bridge because of its many colors. Just this side of The Rainbow Bridge there is a land of meadows, hills and valleys with lush green grass.

When a beloved pet dies, the pet goes to this place. There is always food, water and warm spring weather. The old and frail animals are young again. Those who were maimed are made whole again. They play all day with each other.

There is only one thing missing. They are not with their special person who loved them on Earth.

So each day they run and play until the day comes when one suddenly stops playing and looks up. The nose twitches! The ears are up! The eyes are staring! And this one suddenly runs from the group!

You have been seen, and when you and your special friend meet, you take him or her in your arms and embrace. Your face is kissed again and again, and you look once more into the eyes of your trusting friend. Then you cross The Rainbow Bridge together, never again to be separated.

AUTHOR UNKNOWN

Enid earned her Master's Degree in Social Work from Portland State University. She is a Certified Thanatologist and Compassion Fatigue Specialist. She is the author of five published books about the grieving process which span both human and animal loss.

In October of 1986, Enid founded the DoveLewis Pet Loss Support Program. This program is the third oldest, and longest lasting Pet Loss Support Group in America. In addition to facilitating the support groups four times each month, she provides the instruction and materials for the Memorial Art Workshops for the public on the second Sunday of each month, and for the DoveLewis staff one week each month.

Enid is a pioneer and expert in the pet bereavement field. She speaks locally and nationally at conferences, on radio and TV. Enid is also an accomplished artist; her beautiful glass art decorates the lobby of DoveLewis' main hospital in Portland, Oregon.

Enid is thankful for her husband David, her human children Noah and Maya and for her menagerie of critter children who surround her with their buoyant spirits and unconditional love.

PHOTO BY MICHAEL JONES PHOTOGRAPHY STUDIO

Enid Traisman, M.S.W.
CERTIFIED GRIEF COUNSELOR